PRAYING FROM THE MARGINS

GLEN O'BRIEN

Praying from the margins

GOSPEL REFLECTIONS OF A GAY MAN

THE COLUMBA PRESS
DUBLIN 2001

THE COLUMBA PRESS
55A Spruce Avenue, Stillorgan Industrial Park,
Blackrock, Co Dublin

First edition 2001
Designed by Barbara Croatto
Origination by
The Columba Press
Printed in Ireland by
Colour Books Ltd, Dublin

ISBN 1 85607 324 6

Biblical quotations are from the *New Revised Standard Version,*
copyright © 1989, by the Division of Christian Education of
the National Council of the Churches of Christ in the United
States of America, and are used by permission.

Copyright © 2001, Glen O'Brien

CONTENTS

Preface		6
1.	Beatitudes	10
2.	Cure of the Centurion's servant	14
3.	Peter's three denials	18
4.	The Samaritan woman at the well	23
5.	Lepers	29
6.	The Pharisee and the Tax Collector	32
7.	Martha and Mary	36
8.	Zacchaeus	40
9.	The woman with the haemorrhage	43
10.	The lamp on the lamp stand	47
11.	The rich young man	50
12.	The little children and Jesus	54
13.	The Prodigal Son	57
14.	Baptism	62
15.	Emmaus	65
16.	The son of the widow of Nain	69
17.	The Transfiguration	72
18.	Meeting together in his name	76
19.	The vine and the branches	79
20.	In the beginning	82
21.	The Annunciation	85
22.	The Eucharist	89
23.	Who is my mother …?	93

PREFACE

I did not set out to write a book of reflections. As I heard or read or reflected on some passages of sacred scripture I came to see that they mirrored, challenged, questioned, affirmed some of my personal experiences as a gay man. I began to write down my reflections and that is how this book began.

I have been blessed to hear many experiences from close friends. I have taken these experiences also into my reflection and prayer. I have attempted to walk in my friends' shoes and allow passages of scripture come to mind which take up their experiences. I have decided for consistency and ease of reading to write these experiences also in the first person. I trust that in doing so and in the resulting reflections I do justice to them. All the reflections are written from the standpoint of a gay man. Undoubtedly some aspects of them may resonate with lesbians and with those who are not gay, others may not.

Prayerful reflection tends to open us up to ourselves, to others and to God. It can render us vulnerable and it can render us whole. These reflections are not offered as prescriptive in any way. They may encourage the reader in his/her own prayerful reflection, no matter what his/her sexual orientation, no matter what his/her church tradition or belief. As a Roman Catholic my reflections arise from within that tradition which I know and love. In writing these reflections I stand in God's presence joyfully and assertively. In so doing, I am profoundly conscious that my standing there is God's pure gift. I am conscious also that any attempt on my part to bear fruit in that giftedness is God's pure gift too. In my understanding of the divine-human love story it is not a matter of 60/40 or any other proportion. It is a case of the One becoming Itself in giving and the other becoming itself in receiving.

Throughout the book the standpoint I take is that as a Christian I stand with other Christians as God's People, the church. I refer frequently to the abuses perpetrated over the centuries against gay men and women. In these instances, when I use the word 'church' I mean something rather different, i.e. those in authority responsible for official church teaching and also responsible in various ways for attitudes and actions towards gay people which have caused the grave loss of human and spiritual dignity, human rights, human happiness and fulfilment, and in many cases the murderous loss of life itself, including suicide. In my understanding, this 'church' stands greatly in need of redemption in respect of men and women who are homosexual.

Being gay is not easy and though at times you may feel like cheering about it, you will think twice. I would like to express sincerest thanks to those whom it is a blessing and a joy for me to have as my own family, my friends, companions and colleagues. I am grateful for their constant love, understanding, support and encouragement. They know me and they know my light and my dark sides. I am sorry for the hurt and the loss that my being gay has caused some of them in particular.

I am grateful to Seán O Boyle and his team at Columba Press. Seán responded very positively when I sent him the original manuscript and I have received continuous support and encouragement from him. Without him and his team this book would still be 'standing far off' like the tax collector in reflection number 6. For both Columba Press and myself this book required a certain act of faith and courage.

I hope that these reflections may add a little to the dialogue that gay Christians seek with nongay Christians and their churches. We too are made in God's image and likeness and stand in that good company. Very, very many who stood in that good company in the recent, and not so recent, past have been killed or have committed suicide because of their sexual orientation. In companionship with them and in their memory I offer these reflections. I pray that their joy is complete.

I would welcome your responses to these reflections. Please send them to me at my email address: glenobrien@hotmail.com

1 Beatitudes: *Choices and celebrations*

When Jesus saw the crowds, he went up the mountain; and after he sat down, his disciples came to him. Then he began to speak, and taught them, saying:

'Blessed are the poor in spirit, for theirs is the kingdom of heaven.

Blessed are those who mourn, for they will be comforted.

Blessed are the meek, for they will inherit the earth.

Blessed are those who hunger and thirst for righteousness, for they will be filled.

Blessed are the merciful, for they will receive mercy.

Blessed are the pure in heart, for they will see God.

Blessed are the peacemakers, for they will be called children of God.

Blessed are those who are persecuted for righteousness' sake, for theirs is the kingdom of heaven.

Blessed are you when people revile you and persecute you and utter all kinds of evil against you falsely on my account. Rejoice and be glad, for your reward is great in heaven, for in the same way they persecuted the prophets who were before you.' (Mt 5:1-12, see also Lk 6:20-26)

Reflection

Lord, we are told that values are caught and not taught. Children growing up need this oneness with their parents to achieve a healthy adulthood. They need to know they are loved and cherished and accepted for who and what they are. They need compassion, encouragement and understanding. In this way they learn to love and esteem themselves and move out to share that with others. When children are repeatedly put down they begin to believe what their parents say of them. Surely this is never your Father's will for any of his sons and daughters, destined and called to be his image and likeness. How blessed are those children who learn in their family to be gentle, merciful, peacemakers, to hunger and thirst for justice and the right use of material goods.

Lord, many young gay men as they are growing up and coming to realise their sexual orientation face great confusion and challenge. So much in the church and society are the opposite of good parenting. They learn about intrinsic evil, grave disorders, a sickness and criminal offences. What chance have many of ever achieving a healthy self-realisation? Many are disowned by family, friends, church and society. They suffer, in the words of Luke, hatred, exclusion, defamation and being reviled.

Lord, when I read the Beatitudes I want to celebrate being gay, being a gay son of God. I know that you knit me together in my mother's womb, that you looked at me even then and your eyes sparkled at your new creation, your new image and likeness. From all eternity you know me, through and through, and I am coming to know you in return and to call you *Abba,* Father. Lord, your choice of name for God, *Abba,* Father, is very telling. It gives us an insight into your own relationship with God and it invites us to follow suit. It must be that it was God's intimate oneness with you, and yours with God, that was at the core of your life and ministry and gave rise to the Beatitudes.

Lord I stand before you wanting, in Luke's words, to leap for joy sometimes and ask for the gifts that you outline in the Beatitudes. Let me place love and compassion before possessions and the bright things of life that can deceive and pass away all too quickly. Let me mourn the injustices against gays and let that mourning increase my gentleness and mercy so that I too as a gay man may inherit the earth. Let me hunger and thirst for righteousness and be one with those persecuted in the cause of right, so that I may receive my place in the kingdom of God. Give me strength to grow in purity of heart, despite the sometimes crushing weight of prejudice, so that I too may see God and live as a peacemaker.

Lord, I thank you for the wonder of my gay being and I claim my place with the sons of God.

2 Cure of the Centurion's servant: *The gift of my homosexuality and the gift of eucharistic ministry*

After Jesus had finished all his sayings in the hearing of the people, he entered Capernaum. A centurion there had a slave whom he valued highly, and who was ill and close to death. When he heard about Jesus, he sent some Jewish elders to him, asking him to come and heal his slave. When they came to Jesus, they appealed to him earnestly, saying, 'He is worthy of having you do this for him, for he loves our people, and it is he who built our synagogue for us.' And Jesus went with them, but when he was not far from the house, the centurion sent friends to say to him, 'Lord, do not trouble yourself, for I am not worthy to have you come under my roof; therefore I did not presume to come to you. But only speak the word, and let my servant be healed. For I also am a man set under authority, with soldiers under me; and I say to one, "Go," and he goes, and to another, "Come," and he comes, and to my slave, "Do this," and the slave does it.' When Jesus heard this he was amazed at him, and turning to the crowd that followed him, he said, 'I tell you, not even in Israel have I found such faith.' When those who had been sent returned to the house, they found the slave in good health. (Lk 7:1-10. See also Mt 8:5-13)

Reflection

I'm sure, Lord, that if the Roman centurion knew that his response would be echoed throughout the centuries he would have been very surprised. It's strange how events can affect our own lives and the lives of those unknown to us. Your presence and your power, Lord, are no respecters of people, places or times. The kingdom of God breaks through in its own time and place and in its own way, as this Roman centurion found out.

It is that same presence and power, that same kingdom of God, that encouraged me to say yes when my parish priest invited me to put my name forward to train as a eucharistic minister. My partner encouraged me also. I'm very glad I said yes as my ministry has enriched my own personal life and my life has brought its riches to bear on the ministry.

In the preparatory course we were told that we must give the members of the congregation the same gracious welcome that God the Father extends to the honoured guests at the wedding banquet of his son. We were told to avoid undue regard for a person's status in the community or for distinctions of class, sex, age or race. Were thoughts like these in your mind, Jesus, when you went with them to 'heal his slave'? As a gay man preparing for the ministry I was able to appreciate these recommendations.

Belonging to a community that suffers much distinction based on sexual orientation I believe I can bring to the ministry a strong openness to and awareness of this attitude of the Father's open and gracious welcome. As in the case of the centurion I believe there should be no boundaries as to who 'loves our people'.

Another thing I learned, Jesus, is that the 'ministry of communion is only for those that can look another person in the eye with comfort and touch another person with ease'. Weren't you just like that! Personal communion, we were told, requires ocular, verbal and tactile contact. 'Dare to let your eyes meet those of the communicant and reflect the wonder of God's love in the eucharist. Dare to let your voice announce God's invitation to the banquet of eternal life. Dare to let your hands touch those of the communicant as they minister God's holy gifts. Dare to let the communicant feel the texture of the bread and of your own hand; dare to feel the communicant's hand. It would be possible to place the bread in a person's hand in a more "antiseptic" way, but at the loss of so much of the human, personal warmth of this moment! There is something especially beautiful about helping people receive communion in the hand. Romano Guardini has written that "the soul's chief instruments and clearest mirrors are the face and hands." Even hands that are permanently soiled (like a mechanic's) are beautiful: they testify that a person's livelihood can be seen in the hands, hands that receive the Lord's saving touch and our reverent one.'

Lord, for me personally, the gift of my homosexuality has heightened my awareness and appreciation of each of the 'dares' above. They parallel so many of my experiences as a gay man, in my life with my lover and with my family and friends. I am grateful that the gift of my ministry and the gift of my homosexuality can find such graced common ground and happily interplay.

And, Lord, I smile to myself every time I think that my parish priest knows I am gay and that I am happily living in a gay relationship and I ask you to bless him. I ask you to bless my ministry and that of all men and women in your church. May our common ministry cause us to reach out to the world, to rejoice when faith is found 'not even in Israel', not even in your people.

(Quotations from *The Ministry of Communion,* Michael Kwatera OSB, The Liturgical Press, Collegeville, Minnesota)

3 Peter's three denials: *The denial of being gay*

Simon Peter and another disciple followed Jesus. Since that disciple was known to the high priest, he went with Jesus into the courtyard of the high priest, but Peter was standing outside the gate. So the other disciple who was known to the high priest, went out, spoke to the woman who guarded the gate, and brought Peter in. The woman said to Peter, 'You are not also one of this mans disciples, are you?' He said 'I am not.' Now the slaves and the police had made a charcoal fire because it was cold, and they were standing around it and warming themselves. Peter also was standing with them to warm himself. Then the high priest questioned Jesus about his disciples and about his teaching. Jesus answered, 'I have spoken openly to the world; I have always taught in synagogues and in the temple, where all the Jews come together. I have said nothing in secret. Why do you ask me? Ask those who heard what I said to them; they know what I said.' When he had said this one of the police standing nearby struck Jesus on the face, saying, 'Is that how you answer the high priest?' Jesus answered, 'If I have spoken wrongly, testify to the wrong. But if I have spoken rightly, why do you strike me?' Then Annas sent him bound to Caiaphas the high priest.

Now Simon Peter was standing and warming himself. They asked him, 'You are not also one of his disciples, are you?' He denied it and said, 'I am not.' One of the slaves of the high priest, a relative of the man whose ear Peter had cut off, asked, 'Did I not see you in the garden with him?' Again Peter denied it and at that moments the cock crowed … The Lord turned and looked at Peter. Then Peter remembered the word of the Lord, how he had said to him, 'Before the cock crows today, you will deny me three times.' And he went out and wept bitterly.
(Jn 18:15-27 and Lk 22:61-62. See also Mt 25:69-75 and Mk 14:66-72)

Reflection

Lord, imagine one of your disciples using insider knowledge to get Peter into your meeting with Annas!

John twice mentions the fact of Peter standing there warming himself! Was it the weather or was it some premonition that Peter had that made him cold? Or was it something to do to make his presence pass unnoticed? Lord, how did you feel when one of your closest and most intimate friends denied you three times? Isn't it sad that what was surely Peter's most treasured possession, his association and friendship with you that was foundational to his whole being, is what he denied and wanted to hide. At that same moment you were stating that you had spoken openly to the world and had said nothing in secret; your most treasured possession, your oneness with your Father, was public.

Jesus, we gay men suffer denial in so many ways too. I am thinking here of a threefold denial – denial by self, denial by family and friends, and denial by church and society.

I know gay men, Lord, who hate being gay with a vengeance. They hate the whole reality of being different, longing that they could be straight, have a wife and a family and along with that the approval and support of their family, friends, society and the church. Their pain and agony may lead them to warming themselves constantly like Peter, doing anything to avoid confronting and accepting their homosexuality. In some cases their lives become blighted by excessive abuse of alcohol and drugs, compulsive and meaningless promiscuity, entering into heterosexual relationships or marriage as an avoidance. Lord, find a way to turn and look straight at these men. Let your look be one of immense compassion, and let it issue an appeal to their hearts to be gentle on themselves. Let them know that you do not disown them. Help me to be you for them.

Lord, so many gay men do not tell their parents, siblings or friends that they are gay. The thought of being rejected, denied, disowned can be too awful to contemplate. Some live split lives and may fail to reach any level of real fulfillment in either. Your grace is frustrated in journeying with them to the fullness of life. Like Peter, they live in fear of being recognised, and of the consequences that might have with their family, friends and colleagues. Lord, we gay men can also deny one other and perpetuate hurt, isolation and homophobia even among ourselves. Help!

And this hiding and denying, Lord, is often multiplied when it comes to church and society. If I offer my services in the church and add that 'By the way, I'm heterosexual', the church would shrug its shoulders and say 'So what?' You know, Jesus, that if I were to add 'By the way, I'm homosexual' the response would be very different. So we perpetuate the denial. The same is true, Lord, of society when it comes to partnerships, employment, housing, clubs, and even in death. Being gay is acceptable if hidden away. Lord, all of this puts great pressure on gay men to deny an integral part of themselves. Like you, we frequently get struck in the face – metaphorically– when we speak the truth of who we are.

Lord, may there be brave and courageous prophets in the gay and nongay communities to speak openly to the world, to bring healing to both communities so that the secret and bitter weeping may pass away. May denial give way to acceptance, and disowning turn into welcoming and homecoming.

4 The Samaritan woman at the well
Truth and inclusiveness

So he came to a Samaritan city called Sychar, near the plot of ground that Jacob had given to his son Joseph. Jacob's well was there, and Jesus, tired out by his journey, was sitting by the well. It was about noon.

A Samaritan woman came to draw water, and Jesus said to her, 'Give me a drink.' (His disciples had gone to the city to buy food.) The Samaritan woman said to him, 'How is it that you, a Jew, ask a drink of me, a woman of Samaria?' (Jews do not share things in common with Samaritans.) Jesus answered her, 'If you knew the gift of God, and who it is that is saying to you, 'Give me a drink,' you would have asked him, and he would have given you living water.' The woman said to him, 'Sir, you have no bucket, and the well is deep. Where do you get that living water? Are you greater than our ancestor Jacob, who gave us the well, and with his sons and his flocks drank from it?' Jesus said to her, 'Everyone who drinks of this water will be thirsty again, but those who drink of the water that I will give them will never be thirsty. The water that I will give will become in them a spring of water gushing up to eternal life.' The woman said to him, 'Sir, give me this water, so that I may never be thirsty or have to keep coming here to draw water.'

Jesus said to her, 'Go, call your husband, and come back.' The woman answered him, 'I have no husband.' Jesus said to her, 'You are right in saying, "I have no husband"; for you have had five husbands, and the one you have now is not your husband.' 'What you have said is true!' The woman said to him, 'Sir, I see that you are a prophet. Our ancestors worshipped on this mountain, but you say that the place where people must worship is in Jerusalem.' Jesus said to her, 'Woman, believe me, the hour is coming when you will worship the Father neither on this mountain nor in Jerusalem. You worship what you do not know; we worship what we know, for salvation is from the Jews. But the hour is coming, and is now here, when the true worshippers will worship the Father in spirit and truth, for the Father seeks such as these to worship him. God is spirit , and those who worship him must worship in spirit and truth.' The woman said to him, 'I know that Messiah is coming' (who is called Christ). 'When he comes, he will proclaim all things to us.' Jesus said to her, 'I am he, the one who is speaking to you.'

Just then his disciples came. They were astonished that he was speaking with a woman, but no one said, 'What do you want?' or 'Why are you speaking with her?' Then the woman left her water jar and went back to the city. She said to the people, 'Come and see a man who told me everything I have ever done! He cannot be the Messiah, can he?' They left the city and went on their way to him.

Meanwhile the disciples were urging him, 'Rabbi, eat something.' But he said to them, 'I have food to eat that you do not know about.' So the disciples said to one another, 'Surely no one has brought him something to eat?' Jesus said to them, 'My food is to do the will of him who sent me and to complete his work. Do you not say, 'Four months more, then comes the harvest'? But I tell you, look around you, and see how the fields are ripe for harvesting. The reaper is already receiving wages and is gathering fruit for eternal life, so that sower and reaper may rejoice together. For here the saying holds true, 'One sows and another reaps.' I sent you to reap that for which you did not labour. Others have laboured, and you have entered into their labour.'

Many Samaritans from that city believed in him because of the woman's testimony, 'He told me everything I have ever done.' So when the Samaritans came to him, they asked him to stay with them; and he stayed there two days. And many more believed because of his word. They said to the woman, 'It is no longer because of what you said that we believe, for we have heard for ourselves, and we know that this is truly the Saviour of the world.' (Jn 4:5-42)

Reflection

Jesus, you were an outsider in Samaria, you did not belong there. Yet you spoke to the Samaritan woman. As you well know, Jesus, not only did Jews not associate with Samaritans but, among other things, under no circumstances would they use dishes that Samaritans used. What total separation! How many in today's church and society would gladly separate us gays from the rest of humankind. Where do you stand, Lord?

Yet, here you are crossing the barrier. What was it that made you feel at ease, at home with this Samaritan woman? Was it your sense of God's spirit in her, a spirit not identified with 'this mountain' or 'Jerusalem'? Her drinking cup was what you sought to drink from; you met her at a very close and intimate level. Such intimacy on your part must have been grounded in an overwhelming sense of your Father's unbounded compassion for and oneness with all his sons and daughters. Lord, give us that sense as gay men so that we may seek and accomplish such intimacy with our nongay brothers and sisters. Give us the courage as 'strangers' and 'outsiders' in society to offer sustenance to and receive sustenance from the 'insiders', to seek to drink openly from the riches of Christianity and its churches. Give us the strength to know that Christianity and its churches were, are and will be enriched by gay men over the centuries, and allow us to play our part in that enrichment and to work toward eliminating outsider/insider.

Jesus, you spoke about giving the water of 'eternal life' and you played verbally with the woman about her husband. It was a game about truth; how difficult is truth! How many gay men can be truthful to themselves and others? How often, Lord, do we have to construct myriads of storylines to keep away from the truth? How many of us have to listen to our straight friends asking about our girlfriends, any sign of the ring or the big day, promising to fix us up with a woman? Some of us would have five wives if our friends had their way, and you know, Lord, that I would have a preference for five husbands!

If eternal life is found in the truth, how do we find it? How many married men find themselves faced with their homosexuality, or some degree of it? How many live 'five' lives at once? How many separate with all the attendant pain and sadness and sometimes tragic consequences, for the sake of 'being true to oneself'? How many ordained homosexual priests also find difficulty in 'being true to oneself'?

Lord, it is difficult to be gay, to be truthful. Sit with me a while as you sat with the Samaritan woman and let us drink together. Let me tell you 'all I have ever done' and open myself to your 'spring of water gushing up to eternal life'. Let your disciples go 'into town to buy food' and when they return let us together enjoy and relish their reaction when they find you sharing a cup with a queer!

5 Lepers: *Touching God in others*

A leper came to him begging him, and kneeling he said to him, 'If you choose, you can make me clean.' Moved with pity, Jesus stretched out his hand and touched him, and said to him, 'I do choose. Be made clean!' Immediately the leprosy left him, and he was made clean. After sternly warning him he sent him away at once, saying to him, 'See that you say nothing to anyone; but go, show yourself to the priest, and offer for your cleansing what Moses commanded, as a testimony to them.' But he went out and began to proclaim it freely, and to spread the word, so that Jesus could no longer go into a town openly, but stayed out in the country; and people came to him from every quarter. (Mk 1:40-45. See also Mt 8:1-4 and Lk 5:12-16)

Reflection

I have always been drawn, Jesus, by the way you touched lepers. You touched the untouchables and in a way rendered yourself untouchable. You touched them, looked into their eyes, you spoke to them. You allowed others to touch you and be healed.

Lord, I too experience the power of touch. My partner and I never fail to be grateful for its extraordinary power and mystery.

Sometimes when I arrive home after a tough day, feeling worn out, his look, his few words and especially his touch seem to reach my very being, to welcome me 'home' almost metaphysically. It seems to draw out my dis-ease and breathe in ease. Such experiences, Lord, I can only call sacramental and in them I know your gracious touch is co-present.

There are times, Lord, when I may be reading, studying, listening to music, on the phone, shaving, sleeping and he passes by unobtrusively and gently touches me on my shoulder, my hand, my face, my head, my body. Such moments fill me with love for him, nourish and sustain that love, that love which joins us together and which we pray will never be sundered. Did you touch your friends, Jesus, to nourish and sustain their commitment to you? You are recorded frequently touching the sick and sinners but surely you also touched those close to you, your followers.

Lord, there are special times when I sense your gentle presence, your touch in my life. Among those are occasions when my partner and I rest, play and love together. They may be celebrations of our love for each other, celebrations of special occasions in our lives, a coming together after a falling out or a row. The overwhelming power of touch at such moments is one of life's greatest gifts. When I reach out and touch him, when his body touches mine, when I reach out and touch his face and eyes, the sacred and the profane merge and I sense the presence of mystery. My whole body can quiver with the power of that touch. It is as if I leave behind this world and enter another, one that transcends time and death.

When I hold his head and face gently in my hands and look into his eyes I experience a joy that almost breaks me. It's like I am holding the face of God in my hands and he is holding mine in his. Such moments for me are linked with sacred moments, like when I hold the eucharistic bread in my hands, aware of the transcendent reality that is breaking through in the immanence of bread. There is for me, Lord, a divine encounter both in the eucharist and in those moments with my partner.

Lord, I am grateful for your touch in my life, in my life with my partner; for its power to draw out love, compassion, hope, vulnerability, understanding, belonging and acceptance. I pray that such experiences send me out each day more aware of your hidden touch in all of life and creation, and more generous in my response.

6 The Pharisee and The Tax Collector
Putting me in my place!

He also told this parable to some who trusted in themselves that they were righteous and regarded others with contempt: 'Two men went up to the temple to pray, one a Pharisee and the other a tax collector. The Pharisee, standing by himself, was praying thus, 'God, I thank you that I am not like other people: thieves, rogues, adulterers, or even like this tax collector. I fast twice a week; I give a tenth of all my income.' But the tax collector, standing far off, would not even look up to heaven, but was beating his breast and saying, 'God, be merciful to me, a sinner!' I tell you, this man went down to his home justified rather than the other; for all who exalt themselves will be humbled, but all who humble themselves, will be exalted.' (Lk 18:9-14)

Reflection

Lord, on the surface of it, two men going up to the temple to pray seems a good thing. Prayer can be a way of entering our deepest being, a getting in touch with who and how we are as persons, a quiet recognition that there is more to life than the superficial.

Prayer can be a focusing exercise too, Jesus, and in your story each man chose a different focus. What a wonderful storyteller you are, drawing such clear and unambiguous characters as in this story.

I can just picture the Pharisee 'standing by himself' with hands uplifted and praying to himself. He thanks you that he is 'not like other people' – if I could suggest gay men to him he would most certainly add us to his list. How little changes, Jesus, in the human condition. There are many such Pharisees in church and society today, still awaiting redemption. There is, to be honest, a Pharisee in me too and I am glad of this parable to remind myself of the need and benefit of regular self stock-taking. Lord, help us all to see that going 'up to the temple' can be a very enriching and joyful experience; taking time out from a busy life to retreat alone and seek reconciliation with self and with you, Lord. Such experiences, either a moment in an ordinary day, or a few days away, can help focus us on the important things in life.

What a magnificent picture you draw of the tax collector. There he was 'standing far off'. How much meaning you cram into a few words! Lord, to us gay men these few words resonate like thunder. Sometimes we feel our whole lives are lived 'standing far off', as if we didn't belong in the community we live and work with. There is always a sense of being 'other'. And in the 'temple' of your church where all refuge is offered, we are placed 'so far off' that we unbelong. Yet we too 'go up to the temple to pray', we too stand among your faithful to hear your word proclaimed, to approach your table for nourishment; yet in our hearts there is always and forever a feeling of 'standing far off'.

Sometimes it is not difficult for us gay men to be humble – to be humbled has been our lot frequently in the past. Today, Lord, I pray for a true sense of humility; a daily awakening of my need for reconciliation with self, my fellow human beings and with you; a fresh sense of my desire to act justly and lessen the injustices I am guilty of; a new awareness of the necessity to live respectfully in balance with all of your creation, so that I may genuinely 'fast twice a week' and 'give a tenth of all my income'.

Lord, 'standing far off' and 'not even look(ing) up', I pray for mercy; knowing with the deepest joy that for you there is no distance, for you there will be the gentle touching and raising of my chin so that our eyes can meet, for you there will be the strong holding of my hand (that beats my breast) in pure reconciliation. May your absence of distance, your look, your touch find a home in me so that I too may be 'justified', may experience my life transformed and be encouraged to approach others and society with the same compassion.

7 Martha and Mary
A celebration of a life shared in love

Now as they went on their way, he entered a certain village, where a woman named Martha welcomed him into her home. She had a sister named Mary, who sat at the Lord's feet and listened to what he was saying. But Martha was distracted by her many tasks; so she came to him and asked, 'Lord, do you not care that my sister has left me to do all the work by myself? Tell her to help me.' But the Lord answered her, 'Martha, Martha, you are worried and distracted by many things; there is need of only one thing. Mary has chosen the better part which will not be taken away from her.' (Lk 10:38-42)

Reflection

You know, Jesus, that John and I have opened our home to many visitors. How good it is to share what is embraced by the notion of home with friends and with strangers. John and I never stop being grateful for our home together.

You too are welcome among us – your presence is with us as we celebrate our good times and make it through the tough times. Your presence helps us unlock the holiness of the 'ordinary' and allow the sacredness of all life to emerge.

This evening, like Mary, I have 'the better part'. John is busy preparing dinner, it's his turn. I can see him through the open door, moving around, busy, and my whole being looks on him with a love beyond telling. The communion that exists between us is so strong. That communion of love has grown over the years and now seems the most natural thing in the world. Except that for us it is naturally sacred also. The mutual giving and receiving in every aspect of our being together has enriched us in so many ways, has shown to us the reality of your presence among us, your love, your touch, your forgiveness, your hope, something that 'will not be taken away'.

He's still busy, while I'm reflecting! Even to hear him sometimes talking, humming, singing to himself as he cooks, the noise of the pots, of the cutlery as the table is being set, all these familiar sounds fill my heart with love for him.

He has a greater artistic sense than I have and I love when he cooks a special meal, prepares the table in a special way to catch a particular moment in our life, in our relationship, in our love. How I love those intimate meals when we break bread together and share the same glass of wine.

Sometimes, Lord, we are both very distracted like Martha and tensions can grow and drive a wedge between us. We have to be open at these times, open to talking and listening, open to sitting down and sharing what makes us 'distracted by many things' or at times angry and explosive. We have been through times like these and your gracious underlying touch in our lives has helped us in our growing together again, in our mutual forgiveness and reconciliation.

Like the home of Martha, Mary and Lazarus, we too have no children. Yet the fullness of our life and love together calls us to celebrate and nurture life with a passion. We long that our love will be life serving and know that it does that in many ways. In itself it builds us up as persons and we bring more integrated selves out into our daily lives – at work, in our social contacts, with our families and in our service to our church and society. I also serve life by my voluntary work with a gay switchboard, helping people who may be depressed, confused or suicidal, people who need to talk about their homosexuality, young people coming to terms with their sexual orientation, the families of these people. Your strength, Lord, helps me through those hours. John is involved with a local youth centre and works with programmes that help keep young people off the street and begin a new life in a home and seek training for employment.

Often, Lord, when we come home from such

work we share our tiredness, share our feelings of anger and upset at what so many young people suffer, upset over so much dysfunction in families and in society. At times like these we recognise and experience, humbly, the joy and fulfilment we have in our life together.

Lord, thank you for the life and the love we share together. Strengthen our love for each other so that we may continue to serve you in the world and not, using Martha's words, leave others to do the work by themselves.

8 Zacchaeus: *Salvation for gay men*

He entered Jericho and was passing through it. A man was there named Zacchaeus; he was a chief tax collector and was rich. He was trying to see who Jesus was, but on account of the crowd he could not, because he was short in stature. So he ran ahead and climbed a sycamore tree to see him, because he was going to pass that way. When Jesus came to the place, he looked up and said to him, 'Zacchaeus, hurry and come down; for I must stay at your house today.' So he hurried down and was happy to welcome him. All who saw it began to grumble and said, 'He has gone to be the guest of one who is a sinner.' Zacchaeus stood there and said to the Lord, 'Look, half of my possessions, Lord, I give to the poor; and if I have defrauded anyone of anything, I will pay back four times as much.' Then Jesus said to him, 'Today salvation has come to this house, because he too is a son of Abraham. For the Son of Man came to seek out and to save the lost.'(Lk 19:1-10)

Reflection

Lord, so many things in this story leap out at me.

Zacchaeus … his boldness to climb a tree; to be exposed; to be seen even though a 'sinner', a minority, not like the rest; his willingness to help the poor, to pay back those he may have cheated.

Your own reaction … 'Hurry, I must stay at your house today.' Why the urgency of 'Hurry' and the insistence of 'I must'; your statement, 'He too is a son of Abraham'?

As a gay man, Lord, am I willing to climb the tree, willing to be seen and known for who and what I am? Am I willing to climb the tree and seek my rights as a human being, to climb the tree against injustices perpetrated against homosexuals in legislation, housing, employment, long term relationships/ unions, registering partnerships, inheritance taxes, insurances, adoption …?

Lord, when will the church call me down and want to stay at my house? Am I not continuously a stranger in your house, secretly being what I'm not? Zacchaeus came down at once and welcomed you gladly. How I long to do likewise, but that's only dreaming … why am I not free to welcome you publicly as Zacchaeus did?

Lord, you know many of my brothers and sisters

welcome you in their gay lives. Like Zacchaeus they too take on some responsibility for the poor and marginalised, living and knowing in their own lives what being poor and marginalised means; how many heroic and saintly lives are unscripted because the love and sacrifice are hidden away in an HIV/AIDS context? In many of those tragic lives and awful deaths, Lord, is it not true that you issue the same invitation that you issued to Zacchaeus and that it is responded to with immense agony and love … 'I must stay at your house today'?

How often still you find yourself the guest of a 'sinner'. How often still does salvation come to a house, the house of a gay son or daughter of Abraham, thanks to the Son of Man who finds that which is 'lost', lost to the church and to society. Lord, I pray that you will stay at my house today and every day; that your presence will give me the courage to seek a more just life for gay people.

9 The woman with the haemorrhage
A healing touch towards openness and wholeness

As he went the crowds pressed in on him. Now there was a woman who had been suffering from haemorrhages for twelve years; and though she had spent all she had on physicians, no one could cure her. She came up behind him and touched the fringe of his clothes, and immediately her haemorrhage stopped. Then Jesus asked, 'Who touched me?' When all denied it, Peter said, 'Master, the crowds surround you and press in on you.' But Jesus said, 'Someone touched me; for I noticed that power had gone out from me.' When the woman saw that she could not remain hidden, she came trembling; and falling down before him, she declared in the presence of all the people why she had touched him, and how she had been immediately healed. He said to her, 'Daughter, your faith has made you well; go in peace.'

(Lk 8:43-48. See also Mt 9:18-26 and Mk 5:21-43)

Reflection

Lord, this has always been one of my favourite stories. It touches the essence of the mystery that is at the heart of the cosmos, the power of the Creator breathing away in all things. This power, this mystery invites and attracts, it fascinates us, it works in ways beyond our understanding, beyond our grasp. It is something that I am conscious of in my own life, it creates in me a sense of joy at my own being. I feel one with it, it brings me ease and peace, the peace you spoke of to this amazing woman. She obviously sensed it very strongly in you and when she reached out this power changed her life.

Lord, so many gay men feel this power is beyond their reach, that the power itself denies them or is denied them by experiences over the centuries. Can you blame them, Lord? For many of us, our self-esteem is so absent that it gives way to self-loathing and we arrive at a place where our faith is frozen. In this place we have lost our ability to reach out and seek that healing peace which this woman was rewarded with so richly. Because of this, Lord, these men never hear you ask of them 'Who touched me?' They have never been told that they may touch you, seek that healing, or if they have, Lord, the conditions attached to their quest have been life/soul threatening and beyond endurance. Lord, are you angry that so many gay men over the centuries have been denied that power and that that power has returned to you empty? Must your power await fruitfulness until these men enter death?

I have some sympathy always for this woman, Jesus, in the way (in a sense) you make a show of her in front of the crowds that almost crushed you. I picture her as a very strong woman who went her way bravely and quietly bearing her physical suffering as well as the many social and religious stigmas that attached to her sickness. She sought your power discreetly, because her very presence in the crowd made the people who came into contact with her unclean. What she risked for wholeness and healing! And then the overpowering joy of being healed, followed by her seeing that 'she could not remain hidden' and coming 'trembling and falling down before' you. And then she told her story and heard you tell her to 'go in peace'. Lord, so much of this has powerful resonances for gay men. We find ourselves present in groups or crowds of people. They don't know we're gay. Sometimes we may wish we weren't so that we could be fully 'one of them'. How often we say in our hearts, 'If they only knew they would walk away or push me away.' Such thoughts must have been in this woman's mind, Lord, the day she met you. So many gay men deny or anaesthetise their homosexuality because they know that many others consider it a 'sickness', and they don't wish to 'come out' because of the social and religious stigmas attached to being gay. Some live lives of quiet dis-ease and despair, never fully arriving 'home' in themselves. They are in constant haemorrhage like this woman, and your power, Lord, in their lives is shut down.

Many of us long to tell our stories (unlike/like this woman?), long to know that we too may touch you and be healed; long for the day when as gay men we can walk with the crowds without the stigmas of church and society denying your power.

Lord, awaken our faith in you, a faith that will heal us and send us forth in peace to walk humbly and creatively before you in public.

10 The lamp on the lamp stand: *An awful journey to self-knowledge in marriage*

No one after lighting a lamp puts it under the bushel basket, but on the lampstand, and it gives light to all in the house ... For nothing is hidden that will not be disclosed, nor is anything secret that will not become known and come to light ... Let anyone with ears to hear listen!
(Mt 5:15, Lk 8:17 and Mk 4:21-23)

Reflection

Lord, when I read these words I think of my life and the awful journey I made a number of years ago and of the light and the dark side of that journey.

I was happily married for many years and the love of that marriage and relationship bore the blessing of children. Like any marriage, it had its highs and lows, its moments of joy and pain, its moments of intense grace.

However, Lord, I did not expect the earthquake that occurred some years ago. In therapy I made the journey of a lifetime, a journey which involved the light of my homosexuality moving from 'under the bushel basket' to a place on top of 'the lampstand'. This light had remained 'hidden' in my past and, for whatever reason, I was now confronted with an essential truth that lay at the very core of my being.

You know, Jesus, that the short journey from 'under the bushel basket' to 'on the lamp-stand' was like an earthquake. The deepest foundations of my soul moved and their presence became known to me in a way that had remained unknown before. It was as if there was no darkness in me anymore; the truth of my homosexuality was like a light that shone into the deepest corners of my being and I became transparent to myself.

But, Lord, at what cost that transparency! The foundations that made their presence felt are so fundamental that they made the whole fabric, structure and reality of my married life crumble beyond belief. Over a period of months everything that had been precious and central to my married life fell apart with the aftershocks of the earthquake. The 'newly discovered' foundations could not sustain and nourish my life as a married man. It was as if the jigsaw of my marriage had been undone and the pieces had changed so fundamentally that they no longer represented anything previously held dear.

There followed months and oceans of pain for myself and my wife and that pain does not go away. I cannot begin to imagine the suffering and pain she underwent and lives with each day. She is remarkbly compassionate and courageous and I ask your continued strong and gracious presence for her journey. My children too have undergone their own ocean of pain and we are slowly building renewed relationships. I thank you, Lord, for all their love, understanding and courage and I ask forgiveness for all the pain I have caused. After separation, nurturing relationships and friendships that have gone through such a change must be one of life's saddest and greatest challenges.

Lord, I pray earnestly that young gay men today may achieve open transparency and acceptance within themselves and within society and the church so that many marriage partners and families may not suffer either the tragedy above or the tragedy of people living several secret lives.

11 The rich young man: *How hard it is for a gay man to enter the kingdom of heaven ... True?*

As he was setting out on a journey, a man ran up and knelt before him, and asked him, 'Good Teacher, what must I do to inherit eternal life?' Jesus said to him, 'Why do you call me good? No one is good but God alone. You know the commandments: "You shall not murder; You shall not commit adultery; You shall not steal; You shall not bear false witness; You shall not defraud; honour your father and mother".' He said to him, 'Teacher I have kept all these since my youth.' Jesus, looking at him, loved him and said, 'You lack one thing; go, sell all what you own, and give the money to the poor, and you will have treasure in heaven; then come, follow me.' When he heard this, he was shocked and went away grieving, for he had many possessions.

Then Jesus looked around and said to his disciples, 'How hard it will be for those who have wealth to enter the kingdom of God!' And the disciples were perplexed at these words. But Jesus said to them again, 'Children, how hard it is to enter the kingdom of God! It is easier for a camel to go through the eye of a needle than for a someone who is rich to enter the kingdom of God.' They were greatly astounded and said to one another, 'Then who can be saved?' Jesus looked at them and said, 'For mortals it is impossible, but not for God; for God all things are possible ... But many who are first will be last, and the last will be first.' (Mk 10:17-27, 31. See also Mt 19:16-30 and Lk 18:18-30)

Reflection

Lord, what a complex story!

A dramatic scene – you starting on your way, the young man running up to you with a question of ultimate meaning. What a strange response you gave: 'No-one is good except God alone.' What does that mean for gays and nongays?

What an extraordinary young man he was. How many of us could respond as he did, 'All these I have kept since I was a boy'? And yet I know gay men who are like him. Many of them because of their circumstances care for and honour their ageing parents, sacrifice their lives for them in small and great ways, bring their distinctive intuition, empathy and compassion to bear on relationships that can be unbearable at times. Many gay men in such situations experience the utter foresakeness that you felt on the cross, and when they cry aloud their anguish is doubled by their awareness that, being gay, they are less likely to receive support and understanding. It is as if the church has abandoned them. And yet for this young man you 'looking at him, loved him'. Do you look at and love those gay men who care for their parents, whose siblings feel it is 'only good for you', will 'keep you out of mischief', 'on the straight and narrow'? Lord, move earth and heaven so that your church will look at and love these men.

Lord, let me turn the next part of the story upside down, something you were fond of doing when certain people tried to catch you out.

Many gay men live good lives described by you in your quotations from Exodus and Leviticus, but they know that the dividing line for them is not having 'great wealth' but their being gay. They sense that if only they could 'give up being gay' they would have treasure in heaven. This message, implicit or explicit, causes so many of us to experience what this young man experienced, 'When he heard this he was shocked and went away grieving.'

Is it hard, Lord, for a gay man to 'enter the kingdom of God'? Do you look at me, a gay man, and love me? I know that you do and I return that love. But for many it seems that the kingdom of God excludes homosexuals, such has been the teaching and practice of your church over the centuries.

Lord, let them in particular hear your words, 'For

God all things are possible' and let us work together to fulfil your kingdom now and in the hereafter. Let your paradox become a reality now – many who are first will be last and the last will be first – and may the last and the first meet you on your journey, break bread and inherit eternal life together.

12. The little children and Jesus
The nightmare of being other

People were bringing little children to him in order that he might touch them; and the disciples spoke sternly to them. But when Jesus saw this, he was indignant and said to them, 'Let the little children come to me; do not stop them; for it is to such as these that the kingdom of God belongs. Truly I tell you, whoever does not receive the kingdom of God as a little child will never enter it.' And he took them up in his arms, laid his hands on them, and blessed them. (Mk 10:13-16. See also Mt 19:13-15 and Lk 18:15-17)

Reflection

Lord, I am a young man writing a letter before I take my life.

Since I was a young child I have known I was different. I couldn't put words on it but I knew I was different from the other boys. It wasn't a happy place to be and as I grew older I felt left out. I was gay but had no understanding of that. Looking back now I know that everybody knew I was gay except me. But they wouldn't tell me what they thought; they just whispered about it among themselves. And of course they made sure that I was kept away from anything and anyone like me, the theory being that if you don't ever see it, it doesn't exist and therefore you can't become it. They said I was artistic and creative, avoiding the fact that to myself and to others being creative in my case did entail being a fag, second-class or second rate.

As I grew older and more aware of my sexuality, life became even more horrific. The other kids, Lord, made such fun of anything gay, told jokes that made me squirm, behaved towards others à la gay in such fashion as to proclaim loudly that being gay is totally unacceptable and un-cool. My life became a nightmare. My parents and siblings seem to have bought into this attitude, my teachers and schoolmates also – there was nobody I could turn to, nobody to talk to, no one to be at ease with. Not even you, Lord – after all your church looked on me with the ultimate sternness and horror, with the momentum of centuries of prejudice.

My self-esteem doesn't exist. How could it? My deepest longings, my deepest dreams and desires, to love myself and to find someone to love, is considered intrinsically evil. I am the ultimate stranger, the ultimate one rebuked. And I do not find in my life your indignance at such rebukes. I do not hear the words, 'Let him come to me and do not stop him.'

Do I not belong also in the kingdom of God? I cannot go on, Jesus. I pray to be taken up in your arms, to have your hands laid on me and to have you bless me as I enter your kingdom of belonging and love.

I join the many other young gay men whose sexuality became unbearable because of the inability of your church and society to welcome and embrace 'strangeness' and 'otherness'.

13 The Prodigal Son
Being a priest and being gay

Then Jesus said, 'There was a man who had two sons. The younger of them said to his father, "Father, give me the share of the property that will belong to me." So he divided his property between them. A few days later the younger son gathered all he had and travelled to a distant country, and there he squandered his property in dissolute living. When he had spent everything, a severe famine took place throughout that country, and he began to be in need. So he went and hired himself out to one of the citizens of that country, who sent him to his fields to feed the pigs. He would gladly have filled himself with the pods that the pigs were eating; and no one gave him anything. But when he came to himself he said, 'How many of my father's hired hands have bread enough and to spare, but here I am dying of hunger! I will get up and go to my father, and say to him, "Father I have sinned against heaven and before you; I am no longer worthy to be called your son; treat me like one of your hired hands." So he set off and went to his father. But while he was still far off, his father saw him and was filled with compassion; he ran and put his arms around him and kissed him. Then the son said to him, "Father, I have sinned against heaven and before you. I am no longer worthy to be called your son." But the father said to his slaves, 'Quickly bring out a robe – the best one – and put it on him; put a ring on his finger and sandals on his feet. And get the fatted calf and kill it and let us eat and celebrate; for this son of mine was dead and is alive again; he was lost and is found." And they began to celebrate.

'Now his elder son was out in the fields and when he came and approached the house, he heard music and dancing. He called one of the slaves and asked what was going on. He replied, "Your brother has come, and your father has killed the fatted calf, because he has got him back safe and sound." Then he became angry and refused to go in. His father came out and began to plead with him. but he answered his father, "Listen! For all these years I have been working like a slave for you and I have never once disobeyed your command; yet you have never given me so much as a young goat so that I might celebrate with my friends. But when this son of yours came back, who has devoured your property with prostitutes, you killed the fatted calf for him!" Then the father said to him, "Son, you are always with me, and all that is mine is yours. But we had to celebrate and rejoice, because this brother of yours was dead and has come to life; he was lost and has been found".' (Lk 15:11-32)

Reflection

There is no doubt, Jesus, that your stories reach into a myriad of nooks and crannies in people's lives throughout the ages. This one must have as many interpretations as there are people who have read and reflected on it.

In the case of a friend of mine, it mirrors so much of his life in the past few years. As a priest he had been aware of his homosexuality at some level for a long time. But it seemed to have its resting or hiding place somewhere in his psyche. This is how he told me his story:

'For many years I was very happy in my ministry, like the younger brother must have been on his father's property. I remember the enthusiasm I experienced when I decided to study and prepare for the priesthood. I remember the challenges during those seven years and how my joy and determination grew as the years passed. During the retreat prior to ordination I was conscious of my homosexuality but knew it had its quiet place in my life and there it would stay.

I will never forget the joy of celebrating the eucharist for the first time and especially the giving of the traditional 'first blessing'. When I laid hands on the heads of my parents, my brothers and sisters and my friends, it was an experience that confirmed my decision to commit my life to ministry.

Life and ministry were good for many years but something in me said that my homosexuality couldn't simply be ignored. Two summers ago I decided for better, for worse, to take a long holiday abroad for some months and during that time I 'squandered (God's) property in dissolute living'. I let myself go to such an extent that I denied the very basis of my life up to that time. I disowned my past as did the prodigal son when he minded pigs, something anathema to a Jew.

I came back to my ministry in utter confusion. One thing I was sure of was that I did not want to live my life as I did for those few months. The other thing I was sure of was that my life and ministry could never be the same again. I came to God, broken but somehow real, and for the first time in my life I stood before him utterly transparent. I could see through myself as God had always seen through me. And in my brokeness I experienced him as a tremendous lover.'

It seemed, Lord, you were calling him to a new ministry, a ministry to gay people. After a lot of soul-searching he left the official ministry of the priesthood and is now working with gay men living with HIV/AIDS. There is no one special in his life but he tells me that if someone comes along he will enhance his life and his ministry.

We are all on a journey, Lord, a kind of mystery tour and in our lifetimes some of us make the prodigal journey several times. But I know, Lord, that like the 'prodigal father' you hold us always in your sights, with compassion, ready permanently to run, put your arms around us and kiss us, if we even so much as cast a glance in your direction.

As for the older brothers, Lord, like you, they are with us always. Bless them.

14. Baptism: *Being held unconditionally in the arms of God*

They brought him up to Jerusalem to present him to the Lord ... Now there was a man in Jerusalem whose name was Simeon; this man was righteous and devout, looking forward to the consolation of Israel, and the Holy Spirit rested on him. It had been revealed to him by the Holy Spirit that he would not see death before he had seen the Lord's Messiah. Guided by the Spirit, Simeon came into the Temple; and when the parents brought in the child Jesus, to do for him what was customary under the law, Simeon took him into his arms and praised God, saying:

'Master, now you are dismissing your servant in peace,
according to your word;
for my eyes have seen your salvation,
which you have prepared in the presence of all peoples,
a light for revelation to the Gentiles
and for glory to your people Israel.'
(Lk 2:22-32)

Reflection

Lord, recently my grandnephew was christened and it was a very special occasion. Somehow when the focus is on the arrival and baptism of a new baby, the differences among the adults seem to melt away – grandparents, parents, aunts, uncles, cousins all crowd around the infant. In one sense, parents and those not parents, single people and those in relationships, homosexual and heterosexual, these distinctions are out of the focus and take a back seat.

Yet, each one has his/her own story, Lord, which on these family occasions whispers its own happy or sad biography in the background.

On this occasion for me there was a moment of magic, a moment of intense grace, and this is what I wish to reflect on now, Lord. My sister and her husband know I'm gay and I knew in telling them that they would find it difficult to come to terms with. They have been brave and understanding and I know that they now love me nonetheless for who and what I am. Their love for me, Lord, in this situation, tells me again of your love and acceptance of me and of the salvation you have prepared for me.

Anyway, at the party after the christening the baby was being passed around, as is the custom. Part of me, because of some residual doubt of my value as a gay person (how many others suffer tons of this because of you church's teaching and attitude), did not expect or seek to have the infant passed to me. Oh me of little faith, Lord! My sister with the child in her arms at one stage deliberately crossed the room and presented him to me. I spent the next few minutes on an emotional roller coaster. I held this newborn boy in my arms, a new image and likeness of his creator, the beginning of a never ending love story with his Maker. My heart and my eyes filled up with a prayer for his well-being, for a life of wholeness for him. It was a moment of grace, one of those moments when something breaks through in the commonplace and you lose all sense of limits. I was so grateful to my sister for giving this moment of joy to me, for entrusting her first grandchild into the arms of her gay brother.

Dear Jesus, I pray and long for the day when those responsible for 'teaching' in your church will come to know and accept that as I held that infant, as Simeon held the infant Jesus, so too do you hold me and every gay man in your arms unconditionally.

15 Emmaus
A journey, breaking word and bread together

Now on that same day two of them were going to a village called Emmaus, about seven miles from Jerusalem, and talking with each other about all these things that had happened. While they were talking and discussing, Jesus himself came near and went with them, but their eyes were kept from recognising him. And he said to them, 'What are you discussing with each other while you walk along?' They stood still, looking sad. Then one of them, whose name was Cleopas, answered him, 'Are you the only stranger in Jerusalem who does not know the things that have taken place there in these days?' He asked them, 'What things?' They replied, 'The things about Jesus of Nazareth, who was a prophet mighty in deed and word before God and all the people, and how our chief priests and leaders handed him over to be condemned to death and crucified him. But we had hoped that he was the one to redeem Israel. Yes, and besides all this, it is now the third day since these things took place. Moreover, some women of our group astounded us. They were at the tomb early this morning, and when they did not find his body there, they came back and told us they had indeed seen a vision of angels who said that he was alive. Some of those who were with us went to the tomb and found it just as the women had said; but they did not see him.' Then he said to them, 'Oh, how foolish you are, and how slow of heart to believe all that the prophets have declared! Was it not necessary that the Messiah should suffer these things and then enter into his glory?' Then beginning with Moses and all the prophets, he interpreted to them the things about himself in all the scriptures.

As they came near the village to which they were going, he walked ahead as if he were going on. But they urged him strongly, saying, 'Stay with us, because it is almost evening and the day is now nearly over.' So he went in to stay with them. When he was at table with them, he took bread, blessed and broke it, and gave it to them. Then their eyes were opened, and they recognised him; and he vanished from their sight. They said to each other, 'Were not our hearts burning within us while he was talking to us on the road, while he was opening the scriptures to us?' That same hour they got up and returned to Jerusalem; and they found the eleven and their companions gathered together. They were saying, 'The Lord has risen indeed, and he has appeared to Simon!' Then they told what had happened on the road, and how he had been made known to them in the breaking of bread. (Lk 24:13-35. See also Mt 16:12-13)

Reflection

So many stories, Jesus, concern journeys you were on: journeys to and from Jerusalem, up and down mountains, from synagogue to synagogue and here your journey to Emmaus.

So many gay men, Jesus, also spend their lives constantly on journeys. Many never have their own home, moving through life without any still point or centre called 'home'. Many journey through life without experiencing lasting love, a love that to many nongays is unspeakable, and to many gay men its absence gives rise to a life that can be doubly unspeakable in its loneliness and its rejection.

How often, Lord, in our conversations as gay men, when we are joined by straight men, we change the subject of our conversation – we are made to 'stand still, looking sad'. And yet I am often present in straight company and hear humoured banter (some of it beyond banter) of straight men about women! Such banter that arises from heterosexual liaisons is fine but banter about homosexual liaisons elicits a different response.

You listened, Jesus, to the story that the two men told you as you walked along together. They told you about the suspect story from 'some women of our group' concerning your empty tomb and how less suspect it became when 'some of those who were with us (men!) found it just as the women had said'. Are gay men often considered suspect; could they be considered truthful and trustworthy?

Jesus, who do we find to listen to our stories? Your church wants to lecture us but not listen to us. Is my soul different? Is 'Gay' stamped on my soul as a sign that I am perverse and deviant? Does that stamp have a sub-title: 'Once opened, abandon all hope'? Have gays not suffered enough over the years, have they not also a time to enter their glory? Lord, your glory in me must not be suffocated forever.

Lord, we gays need you. We urge you, as did the men on the road to Emmaus, to stay with us. Your broken bread will be in vain if you do not stay with us, encourage us, fill us with your glory. Teach us how to love today and in that loving play our part in realising the presence of Godlove in the world. We too need to recognise you and be recognised by you. We too need our hearts to burn within us as gay men and to be able to say, 'The Lord has risen indeed'. Lord, hasten the day when we all openly break word and bread together, whatever our sexual orientation.

16. The son of the widow of Nain restored to life: *The loss of a partner in death*

Soon afterwards he went to a town called Nain, and his disciples and a large crowd went with him. As he approached the gate of the town, a man who had died was being carried out. He was his mother's only son, and she was a widow; and with her was a large crowd from the town. When the Lord saw her, he had compassion for her and said to her, 'Do not weep.' Then he came forward and touched the bier, and the bearers stood still. And he said, 'Young man, I say to you, rise!' The dead man sat up and began to speak, and Jesus gave him to his mother. Fear seized all of them; and they glorified God, saying, 'A great prophet has risen among us!' and 'God has looked favourably on his people!' This word about him spread throughout Judaea and all the surrounding country. (Lk 7:11-17)

Reflection

Lord, I find it very emotional to write this reflection on Peter, who was my best friend and lover for twenty five years. He died last April, two months before the twenty fifth anniversary of our first meeting.

We lived in neighbouring small provincial towns

and met while out walking one Easter Sunday afternoon. We had both felt lonely on a day when families were celebrating, and took off on a walk.

We began seeing each other and, before long, we fell very much in love. We were much at ease in each other's company and our lives became very enriched by the deepening friendship and love. However, unlike other 'dating couples' we had to meet secretly and privately.

Over the years our friendship was obvious to family and friends but our being lovers wasn't. Abroad on holidays was when we felt totally at home with each other; otherwise, Lord, it was a case of constant vigilance.

When Peter was killed in a car crash I was devastated. I could not share my loss or grief as I knew and experienced it – nobody knew what I was going through or could share it with me. In the church I was just a good friend, another one of the 'large crowd from the town'. It was awful, Lord. I felt doubly forsaken; the love of my life was dead and my family and friends could not share the depth of my loss.

Peter's mother was a widow, like the woman in the gospel. He was very good to her over the years and she misses him terribly. I felt, Lord, that she needed some support and in a strange way we have grown closer. We have spent some long evenings together talking about Peter and, while I have never disclosed our relationship to her, she is beginning to realise that there is more to our friendship than she thought. I take her shopping now and do some things for her that Peter used to do. Somehow I sense his presence around her and around both of us and believe that, in a small way, I am giving him back to her. She is minding my dog while I am on holidays. Thank you.

Lord, I pray for greater sensitivity to each person's life journey, greater respect and understanding in relation to gay partnerships. These partnerships need the support of your church and of society; the support of God looking 'favourably on his people', his gay people. The final death is awful enough; each day should not have the unnecessary death of hiding the joy of a love shared.

17 The Transfiguration
Gay men share the one tent too

Six days later, Jesus took with him Peter and James and his brother John and led them up a high mountain, by themselves. And he was transfigured before them, and his face shone like the sun, and his clothes became dazzling white. Suddenly there appeared to them Moses and Elijah; they were talking with him. Then Peter said to Jesus, 'Lord, it is good for us to be here. If you wish, I will make three dwellings here, one for you, one for Moses, and one for Elijah.' While he was still speaking, suddenly a bright cloud overshadowed them, and from the cloud a voice said, 'This is my Son ,the Beloved; with him I am well pleased; listen to him!' When the disciples heard this, they fell to the ground and were overcome by fear. But Jesus came and touched them, saying, 'Get up and do not be afraid.' And when they looked up, they saw no one except Jesus himself alone. (Mt 17:1-8. See also Mk 9:2-13 and Lk 9:28-36)

Reflection

Lord, I often go walking in the Dublin hills and look down on the great sprawling city. Sometimes I take this opportunity to reflect on my life, and looking down over the city I think of the many gay men there and their journeys to self-understanding and acceptance.

Your transfiguration was part of your journey and also a part of your friends' journey of understanding and acceptance of you. It was a slow journey for them – coming to understand who you were and seeing in you the face of God. The whiteness here tells of your glory, Jesus, the glory that they came to experience and know later in your resurrection and ascension. Your own journey into your glory, Lord, brought you through your passion and rejection.

Lord, as gay men we need to experience a transfiguration, an experience of your true presence among us. For too long we have suffered persecution and rejection with no moments of transfiguration and glory. It seems there is a permanent cloud hiding us from view, banishing us to non-existence.

Yet we too can experience in our lives a high mountain of ecstasy, like the apostles. These moments can occur in the dwelling or tent of our hearts and souls, life experiences where the presence of God is revealed to us in glory; moments when we recognise 'My Son the Beloved' in the reality of our lives; moments when we respond to the words of the Father 'Listen to him'. At such times we hear the words 'you too are my son, whom I love'.

Unfortunately such experiences often remain secret, kept locked in our hearts. Who would believe that in their gay lives gay men could experience such transfiguration, could see the face of God? Lord, how I long to share my transfiguration, so that others might acknowledge their own experiences and hence enrich themselves and your church.

As I look down at the city today, I am angry at the way distinction is made between 'being gay' and 'being actively gay'. Lord, I have never heard anyone make the distinction between 'being heterosexual' and 'being actively heterosexual' in the same way and with the same connotations. It is as if separate tents exist for gays and straights. Surely there is only one tent where your glory resides, and we belong in that tent when we reach out to others in love and compassion, when we recognise our own need of God and his presence and his touch in our lives. Help us, Lord, to 'get up and … not be afraid' and experience how good it is 'for us to be here.'

I welcome your presence in my life. I welcome

your theophany to me in the little things and in the great. Grant that your glory may find a dwelling place in my life and in my loving and that it may return to you with joy, fulfilled.

18 Meeting together in his name
Beware – gay men at prayer

'Again, truly I tell you, if two of you agree on earth about anything you ask, it will be done for you by my Father in heaven. For where two or three are gathered in my name, I am there among them.'
(Mt 18:19-20)

Reflection

I suppose, Lord, that for many Christians the thought of gay men gathering together in your name verges on the sacrilegious or hypocrisy. Yet you know that we too have a spiritual self, one needing nourishment and care. Our faith is nourished like any other, by prayer and reflection, communal worship and liturgy, awareness of and a generous response to the sacred that suffuses all of life and creation, and the issues of justice involved.

While it may be fine to be part of the local congregation where I live, even there I am an outsider. Gays are never mentioned or welcomed at church services. But, as you know, Lord, there are many gay priests and religious, many gay men involved in the ministries. We bring our own gifts to bear on the coming of the kingdom of God.

I find I can truly relax and be fully myself in your presence when I gather with other gay men. There are Christian groups of gay men and I have experienced the great joy of celebrating the eucharist with such groups. These eucharists bring us together in a special way; they build us up in our faith and in our humanity, in our self-acceptance and self-love. They call us forth in freedom as sons of God to respond to your presence and invitation in all of life, to follow your path of compassion and self-giving. They are truly sacramental moments, Lord. Thank you for being with gay men when we gather together in your name.

Jesus, you know also that there are other gay men who long to celebrate and pray in such groups. But for some even these gatherings are risky. A man arriving for the first time nervously is faced with the possibility of meeting someone he knows, a neighbour, a relation, a colleague, a pupil of his. Such 'outing' moments can't be undone. Because of the whole attitude of society and your church, Lord, many gay men are denied the spiritual nourishment of such groups – fear of being recognised, fear of others telling where you have been – even though it's where we 'gather in (your) name'. We have to keep an air of secrecy around us, around those who kindly host such gatherings. Many are concerned about the consequences of being seen – consequences for their families, their friendships, their work places, their voluntary commitments. It's a bit like the persecutions, Lord, in the early church.

Lord, did you ever intend such conditions to surround those who were to gather together in your name?

19 The vine and the branches
Love one another, past lovers and present friends

'I am the true vine, and my Father is the vinegrower. He removes every branch in me that bears no fruit. Every branch that bears fruit he prunes to make it bear more fruit. You have already been cleansed by the word that I have spoken to you. Abide in me as I abide in you. Just as the branch cannot bear fruit by itself unless it abides in the vine, neither can you unless you abide in me. I am the vine, you are the branches. Those who abide in me and I in them bear much fruit, because apart from me you can do nothing. Whoever does not abide in me is thrown away like a branch and withers; such branches are gathered, thrown into the fire, and burned. If you abide in me and my words abide in you, ask for whatever you wish, and it will be done for you. My Father is glorified by this, that you bear much fruit, and become my disciples. As the Father has loved me, so I have loved you; abide in my love. If you keep my commandments, you will abide in my love, just as I have kept my Father's commandments and abide in his love. I have said these things to you so that my joy may be in you, and that your joy may be complete.

This is my commandment, that you love one another as I have loved you.' (Jn 15:1-12)

Reflection

Lord, the other night Jack came to my door, very alone and down. He and I were lovers briefly and we have remained in occasional contact. His life tends to go through periods where he withers away, failing to find some joy and happiness in life, in love. He doesn't find being gay very easy. Few of his friends know he is gay and his family certainly don't. I have rarely seen him in great form and I am sad for him when I read your words 'that my joy may be in you and your joy may be complete'.

There is a sense in which I can say that I love him; our sharing and loving has left us with a deep sense of friendship and, using the analogy of this story, we are both connected to the same vine.

Anyway, the other night when he called, Lord, I really didn't want to give him time. I was 'busy'. But something of the vine and the branches urged me to give him a hug and make him feel welcome. We sat down and over coffee I listened to his most recent love stories and their demise. He wasn't too upset but needed an understanding ear. Is this, Lord, the bearing of fruit, to your Father's glory?

He needed reassurance and, knowing what that is like, I was glad to give it to him. It grew late and he asked if it were possible for him to stay the night and simply fall asleep in my arms. Lord, how could I refuse? Did you choose me that night to be his friend, to stop the withering process in his life?

He fell asleep as soon as his head hit the pillow. My arm across his breast felt his lungs fill and empty and I experienced a great oneness with him in his pain and seeming fruitlessness of life. But I know that he too has been 'friend' to others and I prayed for him and for me that we may always 'love one another' and always remain on the vine.

20 In the beginning
Being gay with God in the beginning

In the beginning was the Word, the Word was with God, and the Word was God. He was in the beginning with God. All things came into being through him, and without him not one thing came into being. What has come into being in him was life, and the life was the light of all people. The light shines in the darkness, and the darkness did not overcome it … The true light, which enlightens everyone, was coming into the world.

He was in the world, and the world came into being through him; yet the world did not know him. He came to what was his own, and his own people did not accept him. But to all who received him, who believed in his name, he gave power to become children of God, who was born, not of blood or of the will of the flesh or of the will of man, but of God.

And the Word became flesh and lived among us, and we have seen his glory, the glory as of a father's only son, full of grace and truth. (Jn 1:1-14)

Reflection

Lord, this is also one of my favourite scripture pieces.

I love the way that what we can only refer to as 'before' or 'beyond' time is seamlessly knitted into time, the transcendent into the immanent. I love the concept of 'word'. Words are constitutive of who and what I am – they attempt to define reality, but reality transcends definition.

You, Jesus, are the Word, God's creative Word. Through you all things, all men and women of whatever sexual orientation, are made.

It never ceases to amaze me, Lord, that God expressed his reality in his Word. He gave expression, birth to that reality in the person of you, Jesus. The Word of God is distinct but not separate from God. Defining Jesus and defining God are not identical. God is not defined in Jesus but, in our understanding, without Jesus the definition of God is incomplete.

Lord, as a gay man I treasure this reading. I too am your word. I too experience in my being and in my living your reality. You become again in my life. From all eternity I was in your Word and in your heart; from all eternity I was there as a gay man. When I became flesh your joy was no less than when nongays become flesh. I too claim to be among the *dramatis personae* of your glory, of your fullness of grace and truth.

How do I define myself, Lord? I am more than my homosexuality, but without my homosexuality I am not defined. All of me was with God in the beginning and all of me is called to be your witness, Lord, to testify concerning the light, to become a son of God.

Lord, you dwell among us in so many ways, in our struggle for justice, for truth. Your dwelling place doesn't discriminate on the basis of sexual orientation. I too as a gay man am your dwelling place, your word made flesh, your glory manifested.

May the joy of experiencing and knowing that fact give me the strength and the grace to recognise that selfsame Word in the face and in the life of each person I meet today, gay or nongay.

21. The Annunciation: *I too find favour with God and receive an invitation to say 'yes'*

In the sixth month the angel Gabriel was sent by God to a town in Galilee called Nazareth, to a virgin engaged to a man whose name was Joseph, of the house of David. The virgin's name was Mary. And he came to her and said, 'Greetings, favoured one! The Lord is with you.' But she was much perplexed by his words and pondered what sort of greeting this might be. The angel said to her, 'Do not be afraid, Mary, for you have found favour with God. And now, you will conceive in your womb and bear a son, and you will name him Jesus. He will be great, and will be called the Son of the Most High, and the Lord God will give to him the throne of his ancestor David. He will reign over the house of David forever, and of his kingdom there will be no end.' Mary said to the angel, 'How can this be, since I am a virgin?' The angel said to her, 'The Holy Spirit will come upon you, and the power of the Most High will overshadow you; therefore the child to be born will be holy; he will be called Son of God. And now, your relative Elizabeth in her old age has also conceived a son; and this is the sixth month for her who was said to be barren. For nothing will be impossible with God.' Then Mary said, 'Here am I, the servant of the Lord; let it be with me according to your word.' Then the angel departed from her…

And Mary said,

'My soul magnifies the Lord,

and my spirit rejoices in God my saviour,

for he has looked with favour on the lowliness of his servant.

Surely, from now on all generations will call me blessed;

for the Mighty One has done great things for me, and holy is his name.

His mercy is for those who fear him from generation to generation.

He has shown strength with his arm;

he has scattered the proud in the thoughts of their hearts.

He has brought down the powerful from their thrones,

and lifted up the lowly;

he has filled the hungry with good things,

and sent the rich away empty.

He has helped his servant Israel,

in remembrance of his mercy,

according to the promise he made to our ancestors,

to Abraham and his descendants forever.'

(Lk 1:26-38, 46-55)

Reflection

Lord, this story always leaves me with a little shiver. As I see it this scene is the locus of the incarnation, the decisive moment when God enters in a unique way into his creation, into history, in the person of Jesus. All of evolution, all of history, reaches a certain climax in this event in Nazareth. What I find staggering is the manner in which you approach us, in the person of Mary, graciously seeking our involvement, our blessing, in your incarnation. It seems that Mary's 'yes' to your invitation is integral to redemption.

Because of your incarnation, Lord, each of us is a 'favoured one' and you are with us as you were with Mary. Each of us is approached by your angel, each with the message that we 'have found favour with God'. As a gay man, this is not a message I hear very often, if ever. Indeed, this message tempts me to reply, paraphrasing Mary's words, 'How can this be, since I am gay?'

But somehow I know that I too am born of God, a son of God and holy. May all gay men and women discover in these words of the angel Gabriel a sense of their own worth, a sense of the invitation to be truly born of God, to conceive God in their hearts and to give birth to that conception in their living and in their loving.

Lord, this message to me, this invitation, inevitably seeks a response. Am I able for it, am I able to respond with Mary's 'yes'? I am scared but I take some comfort from the angel's words: 'Nothing will be impossible with God' and from the words of Mary's *Magnificat* – hearing of my blessedness, your mercy for me, your lifting me up and filling me with good things.

May my 'yes', with Mary's help, find expression anew each day, in each difficult situation I find myself in as a gay man, in each important choice I have to make. May it be strongest when those who are 'proud … powerful … rich' seek to empty me of my favour with you.

22 The Eucharist
A communion of love, poured out

When the hour came, he took his place at the table, and the apostles with him. He said to them, 'I have eagerly desired to eat this Passover with you before I suffer; for I tell you, I will not eat it until it is fulfilled in the kingdom of God.' ... Then he took a loaf of bread, and when he had given thanks, he broke it and gave it to them, saying, 'This is my body, which is given for you. Do this in remembrance of me.' And he did the same with the cup after supper, saying, 'This cup that is poured out for you is the new covenant in my blood.' ...

I give you a new commandment, that you love one another. Just as I have loved you, you also should love one another. By this everyone will know that you are my disciples, if you have love for one another. (Lk: 22:14-20, Jn 13:34-35. See also Mt 26:20-30, Mk 14:17-26)

Reflection

Lord, I love your eucharist and I love celebrating it with family, friends and strangers.

In his book, *Liturgy Made Simple,* Mark Searle says that 'Liturgy draws on all the elements of our lives: our bodies, significant persons, society, and the things we use to sustain and enhance our lives. It teaches us to use our bodies to house the presence of God, to worship him and to serve him, and to bring his word and healing to others. It teaches us to listen to the voice of God in the voice of others, and to receive at the hands of others the gifts of God himself. It teaches us to live in the society of others, people of different background and different race, as men and women committed to peace and unity and mutual help. It teaches us to use the goods of the earth – represented in the liturgy by bread and water and wine and oil – not as goods to be grabbed, accumulated and consumed, but as sacraments of the creator himself, to be accepted with thanksgiving, handled with reverence, and shared with generosity.'

(Quotation from *Liturgy Made Simple,* Mark Searle, The Liturgical Press, Collegeville, Minnesota, 1982, page 27)

Lord Jesus, I thank you for my brother Tony and his partner. They have a love of the eucharist and on the occasions when I have been with them at Mass, I am taken by their reverence. But why should I be, knowing them as well as I do? Their whole lives seems to reflect the 'given up' and the 'poured out' of the eucharist, their living of the 'new commandment' exemplary.

When I read the passage by Mark Searle I am thinking of them. The way they are together, physically, in their bodies, they seem to worship and bring healing to each other. I sense that even when I see them taking holy communion together. Their eyes seem to meet instinctively in returning to their seats. And they bring that healing into the way they are with their friends and with their families.

Sometimes I hear the voice of God in how they speak to each other, how they speak of and to others, how they listen and how they hear, and how they are silent. They seem to create the fulfilment of the kingdom of God here and now, leaving us very happy to be in their company.

They are very conscious at communion of receiving 'at the hands of others the gifts of God himself'. I am not privy to their lovemaking, but their gifting of one to the other in that lovemaking must be the powerhouse in which much of their love is sourced and celebrated, and from which it emanates. Their act of communion in both instances and your act of communion at the Last Supper, are sacred moments beyond words.

I love the occasions when they have parties at home for family and friends. When they 'take (their) place at the table' they share that table and their company with generosity. The pleasure of their food and wine shared, their sense of fun and laughter, their making of their home together a place of welcome and warmth to one and all – all of this points to the kingdom that you spoke of, where your disciples are known by their love for one another.

I thank you, Lord, for the great gift of my brother, Tony, and his partner, Andrew. They are angels. May they continue to accept with thanksgiving, handle with reverence and share with generosity, not only their goods of the earth but also the love they share with each other.

23 Who is my mother …?
The 'will of God' in relationships

Then his mother and his brothers came; and standing outside, they sent to him and called him. A crowd was sitting around him; and they said to him, 'Your mother and your brothers and sisters are outside, asking for you.' And he replied, 'Who are my mother and my brothers?' And looking at those who sat around him, he said, 'Here are my mother and my brothers! Whoever does the will of God is my brother and sister and mother.'
(Mk 3:31-35, Mt 12:46-50, Lk 8:19-21)

Reflection

Lord, you certainly have a way with words. And again we see you looking at those around you, making eye contact as you pronounce the centrality of the 'will of God' in all human relationships.

What is the will of God in relationships, in how we are with one another? I have in front of me the results of a survey of senior students in a second level school. They had been asked to reply to the following question: 'If you and your girl/boyfriend decided to postpone sexual intercourse, how would you let the other person know you loved her/him?'

As a gay man I am fascinated by their replies.

The title they chose for the leaflet produced as a result of the survey was '101 ways to make love without doin' it!'

I wonder if a group of gay men were asked the same question would their responses be very different? As I read them, Lord, there is a lot of wisdom in their responses and perhaps we gay men could listen and benefit from their suggested alternate ways of showing love.

Some have to do with respecting each other's space and this is equally true in gay relationships: Be comfortable in silence together; Give them time to be alone. Lord, you valued silence and time alone. Help us to value them too.

Some referr to quality time together: Share your dreams; Watch sunsets together; Bring them breakfast in bed; When they are tired, lie with them until they fall asleep. Lord, gay couples need quality time also, times when our spirits may meet, when we recognise in our lover the faces of our 'brother ... sister ... mother'.

Making the other feel special features also and I have no doubt that the crowd you looked at felt special when you addressed them in this scene. The students' responses include: Look across a crowded room unaware of the crowd; If Pamela Anderson/Brad Pitt walked by do not look; Tell them that you want to spend the rest of your life with them. Lord, in our gay relationships help us affirm each other the way you affirmed the crowd.

Some responses, Lord, I leave to your imagination as to how they translate to gay relationships: Have personal jokes; Carry them home when they are drunk; Love them even if they like Daniel O'Donnell; Shave each other; Share intimate moments in a hot air balloon.

One response society is not yet ready for, Lord: Hold hands and be affectionate in public!

Lord, I would love to have a mixed group, gay and straight, and pose the same question to them. Somehow I imagine that when they have shared their responses they would say, 'Why do people make such a fuss about gays? What we have in common is so much more important than anything else!'

Lord, help us gay men to know your will in our relationships, give us the courage to live that out, so that we may find you looking around at us and saying, 'Here are my brothers ...'